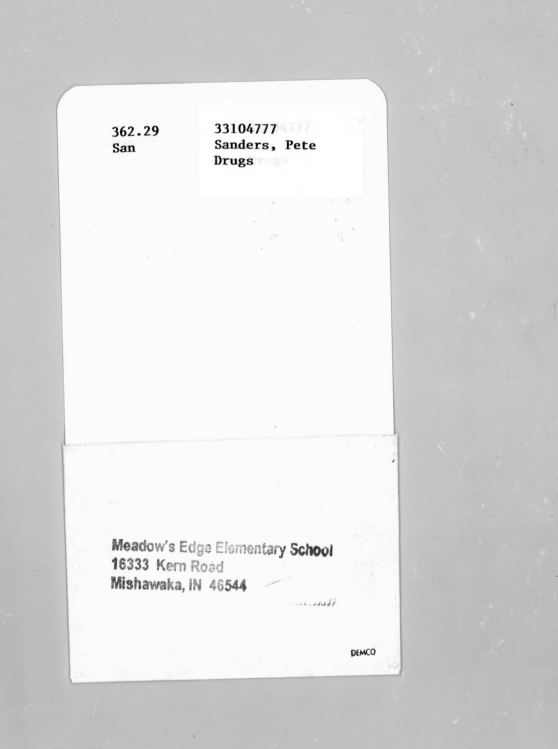

WHAT DO YOU KNOW ABOUT

Drugs

PETE SANDERS and STEVE MYERS

COPPER BEECH BOOKS
BROOKFIELD, CONNECTICUT

Designed and produced by
Aladdin Books Ltd
28 Percy Street
London W1P 0LD

First published in the United States
in 1996 by Copper Beech Books,
an imprint of The Millbrook Press
2 Old New Milford Road
Brookfield, Connecticut 06804

Printed in Belgium

Design   David West
                Children's Book
                Design
Editor   Sarah Levete
Picture research Brooks Krikler
                Research
Illustrator   Mike Lacy

Library of Congress Cataloging-in-Publication Data

Sanders, Pete.
Drugs / Pete Sanders and Steve Myers.
p. cm. -- (What do you know about)
Includes index.
Summary: Aims to provide a better
understanding of drugs and the dangers
of abuse, and discusses what can be done
to help users and to stop illegal use of
drugs.
ISBN 0-7613-0487-8 (hardcover)
1. Drug abuse--Juvenile literature. 2.
Drug abuse--Prevention--Juvenile
literature. [1. Drug abuse.] I. Myers,
Steve. II. Title. III. Series: Sanders, Pete.
What do you know about.
HV5801.S3139 1996
362.29--dc20   95-42436
                          CIP
                          AC

CONTENTS

HOW TO USE THIS BOOK
The books in this series are intended to help young people to understand more about issues that may affect their lives.

Each book can be read by a child alone, or together with a parent, teacher, or helper. Issues raised in the storyline are further discussed in the accompanying text, so that there is an opportunity to talk through ideas as they come up.

At the end of the book there is a section called "What Can We Do?" This gives practical ideas which will be useful for both young people and adults. Organizations and helplines are also listed, to provide the reader with additional sources of information and support

INTRODUCTION

AT SOME TIME IN OUR LIVES, ALL OF US WILL COME INTO CONTACT WITH SOME FORM OF DRUG.

Drugs can be extremely useful. Some are vital in helping people who are ill. However, abuse of certain drugs has become a major problem for both individuals and society.

This book will help you to understand more about drugs and the dangers of drug abuse. Each chapter introduces a different aspect of the subject, illustrated by a continuing storyline. The characters in the story have to deal with situations which you might have to face yourself at some point in your life. After each episode, we stop and look at the issues raised, and broaden the discussion.

By the end, you will know more about the different kinds of drugs and why some people misuse drugs. You will also understand the effects that drugs can have on a person's life, what can be done to help drug users and to stop the illegal use of drugs.

WHAT'S GOING ON? ARE YOU MIXED UP WITH DRUGS? THEY SAY FRANK WILKS DOES DRUGS. IS THAT WHAT YOU'RE DOING?

I NEVER MEANT THINGS TO GO THIS FAR. I CAN'T BELIEVE HE THREATENED YOU.

WHAT ARE DRUGS?

A DRUG IS A SUBSTANCE WHICH, WHEN TAKEN INTO A PERSON'S BODY, ALTERS OR INTERFERES WITH THE WAY IN WHICH THE BODY FUNCTIONS.

This effect may be helpful. Doctors prescribe all kinds of drugs to treat different illnesses. If used incorrectly, however, drugs can be dangerous.

Drugs have been around in different forms for hundreds of years. Some are natural remedies. Others are produced from plants or are manufactured in laboratories. You are probably aware of many of them – perhaps you have drank coffee, or taken a tablet for a headache. The most widely used drugs today are tobacco and alcohol.

Not all drugs have the same use or effect. Some are used to treat illnesses, helping the body to repair itself or helping to prevent disease. Others may be taken because people believe that they will have a pleasurable effect. Some drugs are much more powerful than others. One drug may come in different forms and strengths. The effect of a particular drug may also differ from person to person. It can depend upon factors such as a person's size, age, and general state of health. If someone is not used to a particular drug, the effect may be stronger than on someone whose body has become used to the drug. One person may be able to drink a lot of alcohol without appearing drunk. Another may drink a small amount and still become very drunk.

Many people enjoy an alcoholic drink, a cigarette, or a cup of coffee. These are all forms of drugs.

▽ Lisa and Josh Young were visiting their mother in the hospital. She had needed to have an operation.

HOW ARE YOU FEELING TODAY, MOM?

A BIT BETTER. I HOPE YOU'RE BOTH BEING GOOD FOR MR MARTIN. IT'S VERY NICE OF HIM TO OFFER TO LOOK AFTER YOU.

▽ The nurse arrived with some pills for Mrs. Young.

WHAT ARE THOSE FOR?

THEY'RE MEDICINE. YOUR MOM NEEDS DRUGS TO HELP HER GET WELL AGAIN.

▷ In the car on the way home, Lisa asked about the tablets her mom had taken.

HOW LONG WILL MOM HAVE TO TAKE THOSE PILLS?

THERE SEEMED TO BE A LOT OF DIFFERENT ONES. WHY DOES SHE NEED SO MANY?

I DON'T KNOW, LISA. IT DEPENDS WHAT THE DOCTORS SAY. SHE HAS BEEN VERY ILL.

DIFFERENT DRUGS DO DIFFERENT THINGS. SOME ARE A LOT STRONGER THAN OTHERS.

IT DOESN'T MATTER IF SHE HAS TO TAKE THEM FOR THE REST OF HER LIFE, AS LONG AS SHE'S OKAY.

DOES THAT MEAN THERE COULD BE SIDE EFFECTS?

SMOKING'S BAD FOR YOU, YOU KNOW. WE'VE BEEN DISCUSSING IT IN SCHOOL.

▽ At the Martin's house, Tom, Chrissie, & Ethan Martin were eating dinner.

THAT COFFEE SMELLS WONDERFUL!

△ Mr. Martin said it was possible, but that the doctors would keep a close eye on Mrs. Young.

▷ Mr. Martin lit up a cigarette.

YOUR TEACHERS ARE RIGHT. I HOPE YOU NEVER START TO SMOKE. IT'S A DIFFICULT HABIT TO BREAK. I'VE BEEN TRYING TO GIVE UP FOR YEARS.

SIT DOWN, I'LL BRING YOU A CUP. YOUR DAD PHONED, KIDS. HE'LL BE OVER ABOUT EIGHT-THIRTY TO PICK YOU UP. HE'S GOING TO STOP BY AND SEE YOUR MOM FIRST.

The doctors are giving Mrs. Young pills to help make her well.

A medicine is a drug or combination of drugs which has been designed to treat a particular illness. Some can be bought from pharmacies and other stores. Others are prescribed by doctors, and may contain very powerful drugs.

When a doctor prescribes a medicine for a patient, he or she is taking into account several factors, including any possible side effects that a medicine may have on the patient. It is important that you never take a medicine which has been prescribed for somebody else, even if you think you have the same symptoms. Doing so can be very dangerous. If you do feel unwell, tell your parent or guardian.

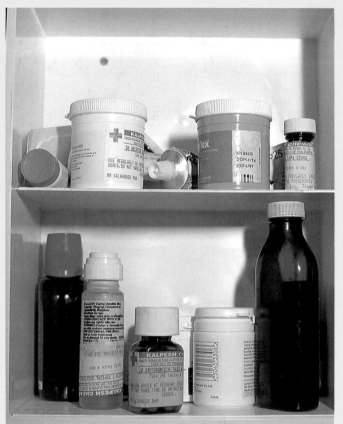

Taking more than the recommended dosage of medicine can be harmful.

Unlike most medicines, some drugs such as cigarettes, coffee, and alcohol do not give a dosage on the package or bottle. But this does not mean that you can have as much of them as you want without any negative effect.

Lisa is worried that her mom may have to take the pills for a long time.

Some people need to take a particular medicine for the rest of their lives. Some doctors have been criticized for prescribing too many drugs unnecessarily. Or they have been accused of repeating a prescription for a patient, without checking to make sure the person still needs the drug.

DIFFERENT KINDS OF DRUGS

THERE ARE HUNDREDS OF DIFFERENT DRUGS. THEY COME IN VARIOUS FORMS. SOMETIMES THEY ARE POWDERS OR TABLETS. THEY MIGHT BE LIQUIDS OR EVEN DRIED PLANTS.

Prescribed or legally obtainable drugs are produced to carefully controlled standards of quality. There are no such safeguards with drugs which are produced, bought, or used illegally.
The effect that a drug has on a person depends on the type of drug, its strength, and how much is taken. It can also be influenced by the method of taking the drug, the situation in which it is taken, the health of the person, and his or her motive for taking it. Sometimes, people take more than one drug to achieve a particular effect. These drug "cocktails" can be very dangerous. Different combinations will affect people in different ways. At the end of this chapter is information about the most commonly used and abused drugs. It shows some of their possible effects, though these will not always be the same for everyone. It also gives details of some of the possible problems associated with each drug.

Drugs which are prescribed by doctors for medicinal purposes are produced and tested under strictly controlled conditions.

WHY DON'T YOU TWO COME ALONG? BRING LISA TOO IF YOU WANT. IT SHOULD BE FUN. IAN'S PARENTS WON'T BE THERE. I'M GOING TO SNEAK SOME BOOZE IN.

IT SOUNDS GREAT.

▷ The next day, Ethan's friend Sam said he was going to a party at his friend Ian's house.

▽ At Josh and Chrissie's school, Josh was upset because a friend of his, Frank Wilks, had been suspended.

THEY'VE GOT FRANK ALL WRONG. HE'S REALLY OK, JUST A BIT OF A LONER.

I HEARD HE WAS DEALING DRUGS. DOESN'T SOUND THAT GREAT TO ME.

WHAT DO YOU MEAN, ONLY "E?" ECLSTASY CAN BE JUST AS DANGEROUS AS OTHER DRUGS.

YOU MEAN YOU'VE NEVER TRIED IT?

EVERYONE WHO'S ANYONE DOES IT, CHRISSIE.

IT WAS ONLY "E," CHRISSIE.

▷ Chrissie said that was nonsense. Josh seemed quite proud.

YOU SOUND LIKE MY DAD. I'M NOT TALKING ABOUT INJECTING OR ANYTHING. AND DON'T YOU DARE SAY A WORD TO ANYONE.

I DON'T TELL ON MY FRIENDS. BUT YOU CAN'T PRETEND IT'S NOT RISKY. DON'T YOU LISTEN TO ANYTHING THE TEACHERS SAY? WHAT ABOUT ALL THE WORK WE DID IN CLASS LAST YEAR?

▽ The school had been doing some work on drugs.

▽ That evening, after school, Ethan, Lisa, and Tom went to the party.

WHAT DO TEACHERS KNOW ABOUT IT?

HERE, LISA, TRY SOME OF THIS. IT'S BETTER THAN PLAIN COLA.

WOW! THIS IS REALLY STRONG. WHAT'S IN IT?

PLENTY. I CAN'T BELIEVE THIS. HOW MANY TIMES HAVE YOU DONE IT?

NOT MANY. LOOK, NOTHING'S GOING TO HAPPEN TO ME.

▽ Ethan told him that Sam had smuggled in some vodka, just for him and his friends.

IT TASTES FUNNY. IT'S MAKING ME FEEL REALLY LIGHT-HEADED.

IT'S SUPPOSED TO, SILLY.

▽ Later, Ethan noticed Sam and his friends Ahmed and Ian sneaking out of the room.

LET'S GO SEE WHAT THEY'RE UP TO. MAYBE THEY'VE GOT SOME MORE BOOZE.

OK, BUT I DON'T THINK I WANT MUCH MORE.

▽ They found Sam and his friends in the garden, hiding behind some bushes.

YOU SCARED ME. GET DOWN, DON'T LET ANYONE SEE YOU.

WHAT ARE YOU UP TO? WHAT'S THAT, SAM?

IT'S GLUE, ISN'T IT? YOU'RE SNIFFING GLUE.

YOU SHOULDN'T DO THAT. IT'S DANGEROUS. COME ON, ETHAN, LET'S GET BACK.

YOU'RE ALWAYS TELLING ME WHAT TO DO. I WANT TO TRY IT. YOU GO IF YOU WANT TO, LITTLE BROTHER.

▽ All three were late returning from the party. Ethan was feeling ill from the glue sniffing.

△ Tom tried to persuade Ethan, but he refused to listen.

WHERE HAVE YOU BEEN TOM? YOU WERE SUPPOSED TO BE HERE HALF AN HOUR AGO. MR. YOUNG'S BEEN WAITING TO PICK UP LISA.

SORRY DAD, ETHAN WASN'T FEELING TOO WELL.

WHAT'S WRONG WITH HIM? HE LOOKS WEIRD.

▽ Suddenly, Ethan ran upstairs saying he was going to be sick.

THEY'VE BEEN DRINKING! THAT'S WHAT'S THE MATTER.

WE DIDN'T HAVE MUCH. WHAT'S THE BIG DEAL? MOM AND DAD DRINK ALL THE TIME.

THE BIG DEAL IS THAT YOU WENT BEHIND OUR BACK, YOUNG LADY. I THOUGHT WE COULD TRUST YOU NOT TO DO THAT.

ALCOHOL • Often drank as beer, wine or spirits • Relaxing effect • Too much will make people "drunk" • Side effects: "hangover" – nausea, headaches, trembling • Acts as a depressant – slowing down the body's reactions • Lessens user's control over emotions & behavior • Can cause damage to the nervous system & liver • Can be addictive • Many deaths each year from alcohol abuse • Legal in many countries but laws control the age at which it can be bought

AMPHETAMINES • Stimulate the body's nervous system and increase blood pressure • Usually taken by mouth – sometimes injected or sniffed • User may feel alert, confident • Can reduce the desire for sleep • Continued usage can lead to irritability; inablility to sleep; anxiety; a fear of others • Also known as "greenies," "speed," "uppers," "pennies" • Illegal to sell or possess • Can be prescribed by doctors

AMYL NITRITE • Clear liquid, used medically to treat heart conditions • Usually supplied in a small bottle • Vapor is sniffed through the nose • Also known as "poppers" • Causes increase in temperature & heartbeat, giving a short-lived feeling of well-being • Continued use can cause dizziness & headaches • Excessive use may lead to blackouts and vomiting • Currently legal

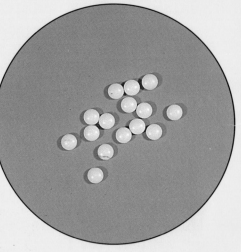

ANABOLIC STEROIDS • Powerful hormones • May be prescribed by doctors for medical conditions • Used by some athletes who believe they improve performance • Can have serious and irreversible side effects on user's reproductive system if not taken under medical supervision • Not illegal to possess, but are a "prescription only" drug

BARBITURATES & OTHER DEPRESSANTS • Slow down certain body functions • Can have relaxing effect & may appear to reduce stress • Long-term use can lead to depression; forgetfulness; increased aggression; an inability to sleep without them; breathing difficulties • Examples of barbiturates include Seconal and Tuinol • Overdose can kill, particularly if taken after alcohol • Tranquilizers are milder depressants – also called "tranx" – examples include Librium and Valium • All depressants can be very addictive • Most can be possessed legally, if prescribed

CAFFEINE • Drug contained in coffee & other drinks, including tea & some soft drinks such as cola • Mild addictive stimulant • Can cause increased heartbeat; heartburn; sleeplessness; upset stomach

CANNABIS • Usually smoked or may be eaten • Comes in solid or leaf form • Also known as "marijuana," "pot," "hash," "grass," "dope," "joint," "spliff & reefer" • Can cause feeling of well-being & relaxation • High dosages can cause vomiting & diarrhea • Continued use can affect people's memory & concentration • Can cause lung damage when smoked • Illegal in most countries to possess or sell

COCAINE • Fine, white powder • Sniffed or injected • Also known as "coke" or "snow" • May create a feeling of well-being & increased energy • Effect wears off quickly – users may take another dose to try to maintain the "high" • If sniffed over a long period, can damage the inside of the nose • Large doses can lead to breathing difficulties and occasionally death • Crack cocaine comes in solid pea-sized lumps which are heated & the smoke inhaled • Known as "freebase cocaine," "rock," or "wash" • Frequent use of cocaine or crack cocaine can cause exhaustion, nervousness & hallucinations • Illegal to possess or sell

ECSTASY • Tablet or capsule form • Known as "E" or "disco biscuits" • Effects include: brief feeling of sickness; increased heart rate; a feeling of calm; greater awareness of surroundings • Has been popular on the dance & rave scene • Causes body to sweat more – loss of fluid, together with the heat of dancing, can cause heatstroke – this can be fatal • Side effects include: diarrhea; tiredness; depression • Illegal to possess or sell

HEROIN • Usually a brownish powder • Either smoked or dissolved & injected • Known as "smack," "skag," or "H" • First effects include feeling of warmth & pleasure • Addictive if used over a period of time • Withdrawal causes vomiting, aches, sweating & tiredness • Dangers from overdose & injecting the impurities which are almost always mixed with street-bought drugs • Possession or sale of heroin is illegal • May be prescribed by doctors medically

LSD • Pill form or as a small piece of blotting paper or sugar cube containing the LSD • Causes hallucinations & altered sense of reality • Effects can be very unpredictable – some "trips" may be unpleasant • Can cause depression; anxiety; panic attacks; dizziness • Also known as "acid," "trips," "cubes" • Illegal to sell or possess

NICOTINE • The drug in tobacco • Can be very addictive • Tobacco comes in leaf form – made into cigarettes or cigars, used in pipes or sniffed as "snuff" • Smoking can cause many illnesses, including cancer & heart disease • Legal to possess tobacco • Illegal for shopkeepers to sell cigarettes to people below a certain age

SOLVENTS, GAS & GLUE • Effects of inhaling vapors of glue, varnishes & lighter fluid can include: dizziness; hallucinations; short-lived feeling of well-being • Can cause nausea; tiredness; headaches • Can cause death from lack of oxygen; inhaling vomit • Legal to possess these products • Illegal for stores to sell them, if they suspect they will be sniffed

WHY DO PEOPLE MISUSE DRUGS?

THERE IS NO ONE SIMPLE EXPLANATION WHY PEOPLE TAKE DRUGS WHEN THEY DO NOT MEDICALLY NEED TO DO SO.

For many people, the reason is the promise of the "high." The high is brought about by the drug and changes the way a person feels or views the world.

This can be an intense feeling of well-being, and may be pleasurable. Because drugs alter the way people feel, they can become a way of escaping temporarily from emotions or situations which are difficult to cope with. Other people may decide to take a drug because they are curious about the drug's effect and want to experience it for themselves. Or it may just be that drugs are easily available.

Wanting to fit in as part of a group can be a strong influence. If others are putting pressure on you to do something, it can be difficult to refuse, even if you want to. Sometimes people have used drugs as the result of a dare. Or they may do it as a form of rebellion, or simply because they believe drug-taking will be fun.

Whatever people's reasons for starting to take drugs, they may not always be aware of what their decision could lead to. Abuse of drugs has the potential to affect your life and health seriously.

Some people take drugs because their "friends" do. They may be worried about what the "friends" will think if they refuse. It takes courage to say no.

▷ That weekend, Chrissie saw Josh with Frank Wilks and his friends in town.

HI, JOSH.

SO WHO'S THIS JOSH? YOUR NEW GIRLFRIEND?

SO, CHRISSIE, DO YOU WANT TO HAVE SOME FUN?

I DON'T THINK SO. I KNOW ABOUT YOUR IDEA OF FUN, AND IT'S NOT MINE.

I'M NOT SCARED. AND I'M NOT A KID. WHAT ARE YOU GOING TO DO?

NO, JUST A FRIEND. SHE LIVES NEAR US, THAT'S ALL. HER NAME'S CHRISSIE.

COME ON, CHRISSIE. IT'LL BE OK.

SHE'S SCARED. SHE'S JUST A KID, ANYWAY. LET'S GO, FRANK.

△ The rest of them turned to leave.

▷ Chrissie was unsure, but she liked Josh and decided to go along with him.

▽ She didn't really want to, but everyone was watching her. She knew she shouldn't, but she took a drag on the joint.

IT'S MAKING ME FEEL SICK.

GIVE IT TIME. IT TAKES A BIT OF GETTING USED TO. THIS IS GOOD STUFF.

▽ They went to an abandoned building, in a part of town Chrissie didn't know very well. Frank produced a cigarette.

BUT I DON'T SMOKE.

IT'S NO ORDINARY CIGARETTE, CHRISSIE. IT'S A JOINT. POT. TRY IT.

GO ON, CHRISSIE. LIVE A LITTLE DANGEROUSLY.

▽ Part of her wanted to go home. She didn't like the way the drug was making her feel. But she was worried about what Josh would think of her.

I TOLD YOU FRANK WAS OK, DIDN'T I? COME ON, STAY FOR A BIT.

IT FEELS GOOD, DOESN'T IT CHRISSIE?

MY HEAD FEELS REALLY STRANGE. IT'S LATE, I CAN ONLY STAY A LITTLE WHILE.

The others are putting pressure on Chrissie to smoke the "joint."
Everyone forms their own opinions of what is right and wrong. If you are part of a larger group, it can be hard to say what you think. If everyone is doing the opposite of what you want or believe is right, it can be tempting to go along with them. It is not always easy to stand up for yourself. It helps to think things through before making a decision. How would you deal with a situation where drugs are offered and you felt under pressure to do the same as other people?

Like Josh, many people who take drugs think that they will be able to control their behavior.
But this is rarely the case. People who have tried drugs may think there are no long-term physical or emotional effects. Or they may believe that somehow they are different – that nothing can harm them. But the reality is that drugs can harm anyone who takes them.

New experiences are part of life.
Trying out different things can be great fun. Some drugs can make you feel good or different for a short while, but there are other long-term and more serious effects which need to be considered. Putting yourself at risk by experimenting, as Chrissie and Josh are doing, is not sensible. It is important to understand the possible consequences of your decisions and actions.

DRUGS AND SOCIETY

THE WAY PEOPLE THINK AND FEEL ABOUT DRUG-TAKING VARIES A GREAT DEAL.

Some believe that the laws about taking certain drugs should be less severe. Others think that legislation is not strict enough.
Sometimes illegal drug-taking is viewed as a problem that happens only in big cities or only to certain groups of people. This is not so. People from all walks of life, of all ages, and from a range of backgrounds can become drug users. Drug abuse is a worldwide problem which affects many areas of society.

Supplying drugs has become very big business. The movement of drugs between countries – "trafficking" – is very risky. Drug traffickers set up very complicated systems, using sophisticated equipment, in order to make their enormous profits. This may involve bribery of officials and even the use of violence. Most countries have very strict laws with high penalties for those convicted.

Different types of drugs have different images. In many countries, alcohol is widely used in social situations. The fact that it is a very powerful drug is often overlooked. Nicotine is a very addictive drug but it is also legal and easily available. Ecstasy has become popular with dancers at raves. Cocaine is often thought of as a "trendy" drug.

Pop and movie stars are sometimes criticized for giving the impression that illegal drugs are acceptable. But nobody is immune to their dangers. River Phoenix died from a drug overdose.

▽ Three months later, Mrs. Young was out of the hospital, but it would be awhile before she was fully recovered.

IS SOMETHING WRONG, JOSH? YOU'VE SEEMED ON EDGE FOR DAYS.

I'VE GOT THINGS ON MY MIND, THAT'S ALL. DON'T WORRY, EVERYTHING'S FINE.

▽ Something in the newspaper had caught Mrs. Young's attention.

THERE'S A STORY HERE ABOUT YOUR FAVORITE ATHLETE. HE'S BEEN BANNED FOR TAKING STEROIDS.

WHAT A CHEAT!

WHAT DO YOU KNOW ABOUT IT? THEY MAKE SUCH A FUSS THESE DAYS.

▽ Chrissie was meeting Josh. She asked her dad if she could borrow some money.

THAT'S THE SECOND TIME THIS WEEK. WHAT ON EARTH ARE YOU SPENDING IT ON?

PLEASE DAD? I'M IN A HURRY. JOSH AND I ARE GOING TO A MOVIE. IT'S MY TURN TO PAY, THAT'S ALL.

▷ Chrissie hated lying to her parents. For a minute she considered telling them everything.

YOU'VE BEEN A BIT DISTANT LATELY. ARE YOU IN ANY TROUBLE, CHRISSIE? YOU KNOW YOU CAN ALWAYS COME TO US, DON'T YOU?

OF COURSE I DO. NO, IT'S NOTHING. EVERYTHING'S FINE.

▽ Chrissie left quickly. She met Josh and Tanya at the end of the street. They went to find Frank.

WE'VE GOT SOME MONEY, FRANK. WHAT CAN YOU LET US HAVE?

NOT HERE, IDIOT, DO YOU WANT TO GET ME ARRESTED? MEET ME IN THE PARKING LOT IN TEN MINUTES.

▽ Ten minutes later, Frank handed over four tabs of Ecstasy.

Some athletes have taken drugs to help them win.

They believe that certain drugs may make them stronger or enable them to run faster. This gives them an unfair advantage over their rivals. At most large competitions athletes are tested for a wide variety of different drugs. If they are found to have used drugs to try to improve their performance, they may be banned from the sport. The most common drugs used in this way are called "anabolic steroids." These can have dangerous side effects.

People like Frank, who make money from selling drugs illegally, are called "dealers." They are also known as "pushers" or "suppliers." Buying drugs from a dealer is very risky. There is no control over the quality of the drug being bought. Dealers may increase the price they charge as the buyer takes the drug more regularly. People can run up huge debts and may turn to crime to pay for their drugs. Dealers may become violent with people who cannot pay.

Most countries have laws about drugs.

These laws may differ from place to place. In England, Australia, and the United States, it is a crime to possess any illegal drug, even if you do not intend to sell it. Alcohol is illegal in some Muslim countries. In Holland and some other countries, people are allowed to buy and sell certain drugs such as cannabis.

ADDICTION AND DEPENDENCY

MANY PEOPLE FIND IT DIFFICULT TO STOP TAKING DRUGS, BECAUSE THEY HAVE COME TO DEPEND ON THE EFFECT OF THE DRUGS THEY ARE TAKING.

Some drugs are physically addictive, causing changes in the body which produce a need for the drug. However, dependence on the feelings that some drugs create, or on the lifestyle and sense of freedom that some people believe they offer, can be just as powerful. If the body has come to depend on the drug, it may crave more of it. Unpleasant sensations – withdrawal symptoms – are felt when the drug is not being taken or when its effects are wearing off. These can be very serious. With some drugs the body develops a tolerance, adapting itself so that a higher dose may be needed to produce the same effect. But this does not mean that the user's body becomes immune to the physical dangers of the drug.

People who use drugs to cope with difficult situations or to relieve unhappiness may become caught up in a pattern. For a short while, the drug will take away the painful emotions but afterward people may feel even worse. The physical effects of the drug wearing off can make people feel unhappy. There may also be a sense of guilt and shame. If they cannot deal with this they may turn again to drugs to escape from their feelings.

Some drugs are much more addictive than others. It is unlikely that anybody who starts to take drugs expects to become addicted. For smokers, the addiction to the nicotine in the cigarettes may become the only reason that they continue to smoke them. The only way to be sure of avoiding addiction is not to experiment with drugs.

▽ Two weeks later, Tom had arranged to meet Ethan after school. When he didn't show up, Tom went looking for him.

▷ Ethan had refused to listen. Later, at home, Tom overheard his parents talking.

△ Apart from the discarded plastic bags, Tom had noticed some used syringes lying around.

◁ Tom went up to Ethan's room. He told him about his parents' conversation.

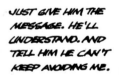

▽ On her way home one evening, Lisa ran into Frank Wilks.

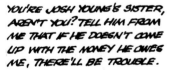

◁ Frank walked away. Lisa hurried home. She felt confused and frightened.

Ethan believes that he is in control.
One of the effects of taking some drugs is to make people unable to think clearly. Their reactions to situations and their ability to reason or to make sensible judgments may be affected. Drugs such as LSD, cannabis, and alcohol can alter people's sense of reality. They may feel powerful and no longer appear to sense pain. Under the influence of drugs, some users have attempted very dangerous activities and believe that they can do impossible things like fly.

Some drug users inject the substance into their veins.
Unskilled injecting is dangerous. It can lead to infections or collapsed veins. If drug users inject with needles that are dirty, they may also be injecting germs into their body, along with the drug. Sharing needles can transfer tiny drops of one person's blood to the other person. If the blood is infected, the infection is also transferred. This is one way in which HIV, the virus which can lead to AIDS, is transmitted. In some countries there are needle exchanges where drug users can discard used needles safely and collect clean needles, unlike in the photo (left). This may reduce the risks from using dirty needles, but it does not help to prevent any of the other dangers associated with taking illegal drugs.

Ethan's parents have noticed that his behavior has changed.
The craving for drugs can take over a person's life, affecting both the drug user and those who are close to him or her. But it can take a long time for others to become aware that a person is dependent on drugs.

WHAT DRUG-TAKING CAN LEAD TO

AS WELL AS THE DEVASTATING EFFECT SOME DRUGS CAN HAVE ON THE BODY, DRUG-TAKING CAN CAUSE OTHER PROBLEMS.

Many drugs alter the way that people behave and can distort their thinking. This can lead to drug users becoming a danger, both to themselves and to other people.

This is one reason why there are strict laws about not driving or operating machinery under the influence of alcohol or other drugs. Depending on the drug taken, the immediate effects might include feelings of power or pleasure. However, there can be serious long-term physical and emotional effects of continued drug abuse. In some cases, drug abuse can lead to death.

Heavy drug users may seem to care more about their drug-taking than about the people who are close to them. This can lead to the breakup of relationships. Friends and relatives may experience a great deal of stress and worry.

If someone is found guilty of possessing even a small amount of any illegal drug by the police, he or she will then have a criminal record for life.

Obtaining drugs illegally can be very expensive. Some drug addicts may turn to stealing, and sometimes prostitution, in order to get the money they need for their supply of drugs.

▽ When Lisa arrived home, she went straight to Josh's room and told him what had happened.

WHAT'S GOING ON? ARE YOU MIXED UP WITH DRUGS? THEY SAY FRANK WILKS DOES DRUGS. IS THAT WHAT YOU'RE DOING?

I NEVER MEANT THINGS TO GO THIS FAR. I CAN'T BELIEVE HE THREATENED YOU.

LOOK, I'VE BEEN TAKING SOME STUFF - "E" MOSTLY. NOW I CAN'T PAY FRANK THE MONEY I OWE HIM. I EVEN STOLE SOME FROM DAD'S WALLET.

YOU'VE GOT TO TELL MOM AND DAD. THEY'LL KNOW WHAT TO DO.

▷ The next day at school, Chrissie went looking for Josh. She was supposed to go with him to a party but had decided not to.

▽ Chrissie had realized how much the drugs had taken over her life. She wanted to stop.

OH GO ON, CHRISSIE. FORGET ABOUT EVERYTHING ELSE. FRANK'S GOT SOME REALLY GOOD STUFF.

△ Josh said he couldn't. He begged Lisa not to say anything until he'd had a chance to try and sort things out.

I DON'T WANT TO DO DRUGS ANYMORE. I WISH I HADN'T LET MYSELF GET INVOLVED IN THE FIRST PLACE. IT'S MAKING ME FEEL REALLY LOW SOMETIMES AND IT'S AFFECTING MY SCHOOLWORK.

IT'S NOT WORTH IT, JOSH. AND I DON'T TRUST FRANK. I'VE SEEN SOME OF HIS FRIENDS - THEY'RE USING MORE THAN "E". BE CAREFUL IF YOU GO TONIGHT, JOSH.

I HAVE TO GO. I OWE FRANK MONEY, AND I NEED TO TRY TO SORT SOMETHING OUT.

▽ There was a shout from behind the two boys. Tanya had collapsed.

JOSH, THIS ISN'T A GAME YOU KNOW. I WANT THE MONEY IN ONE WEEK.

▷ At the party, Josh offered to pay off his debt a little at a time. Frank just laughed at him.

WE'RE SUPPOSED TO BE FRIENDS. WHAT'S GOTTEN INTO YOU?

I'M OUT OF HERE.

SHE'S COLLAPSED! SOMEONE CALL AN AMBULANCE.

Some people think that a person who experiments with a drug such as cannabis will eventually go on

drug, it may be tempting to try another.

This is why it is important to think about what the results of taking any drug might be and to know about the risks involved.

Josh is worried about the effect the drug has had on Tanya.

Illegally produced drugs are not screened for safety. There are no guarantees of purity or strength. The drug that you think you are buying may not be what you are actually given. Taking these drugs is extremely risky. The effect you anticipated may be very different from what happens. It is possible to overdose on drugs. This is when a person has taken too much of a particular drug too quickly. The effects of an overdose can be devastating. It can result in death.

Dealers may take advantage of the drug user's craving and their need for the drug.

They know that many users will not only come to depend on the drug itself, but will also rely on their dealer to supply it. Dealers also need customers. They can be ruthless in the way that they tempt people into starting to take drugs, and then encourage them to continue their drug habit. This can involve people in difficult and even dangerous situations.

KICKING THE HABIT

NO ONE STARTS TO TAKE DRUGS INTENDING TO MAKE IT A HABIT. NO ONE EXPECTS TO BECOME DEPENDENT ON DRUGS. COMING OFF DRUGS CAN BE A LONG AND DIFFICULT PROCESS.

Realizing that you have a problem, and owning up to it, is not easy. Doing something about it can be even harder. But people can and do stop taking drugs.

People are often frightened of what this might mean. For a long time, they may continue to deny that there is a problem. Most people need a lot of help to be able to do without the drug they have come to depend on. Life may suddenly seem very empty without it. Giving up the drug might involve giving up a lifestyle that the person has become used to.

There are various ways that drug users can get the help they need. Some people spend time in the hospital; others may join self-help groups or receive counseling. Sometimes people may not be able to come off the drug completely at once – it

may even be dangerous to try. Under medical supervision, drug therapy may be used to substitute a different drug or to give a lower dose of the same one. In this way, the amount of the drug being taken can be reduced gradually and safely, without the drug-taker experiencing severe withdrawal symptoms.

Telling someone that you have a problem with drugs is a difficult but brave step to take. It can mean coming to terms with feelings that the drug-taking has temporarily blocked out.

▽ The next day, news of what had happened was all around the school.

WHAT HAPPENED? IAN SAID TANYA WAS IN THE HOSPITAL AND JOSH HAD BEEN ARRESTED.

HE WASN'T ARRESTED, BUT HE WAS QUESTIONED. TANYA HAD TAKEN WHAT SHE THOUGHT WAS ECSTASY.

THAT'S AWFUL.

▽ Tom had told Chrissie about Ethan and the glue sniffing. She had talked to Ethan the previous evening.

MEET ME IN THE CEMETERY AFTER SCHOOL. IAN AND AHMED ARE COMING.

YOU GO IF YOU WANT TO. I THINK I'LL PASS.

▽ After class, Ethan stayed behind to talk to his teacher.

SOMETHING'S HAPPENED AND I DON'T KNOW WHAT TO DO. I WANT TO TELL MOM AND DAD, BUT I KNOW I'LL GET INTO TROUBLE.

I HAD A FEELING SOMETHING WAS WRONG, ETHAN. YOU'VE NOT BEEN YOURSELF LATELY. YOUR MIND SEEMS TO BE SOMEWHERE ELSE.

▽ Ethan told his teacher everything.

▽ Mr. Young had spent the previous night at the police station with Josh. They had let Josh go after questioning.

WHY DIDN'T YOU COME TO US BEFORE, JOSH? I THOUGHT YOU COULD TALK TO US ABOUT ANYTHING. WE WOULD HAVE HELPED YOU.

I KNEW TOM WAS RIGHT, BUT I COULDN'T STOP. I FEEL SO MIXED UP. CAN YOU HELP ME?

IT MUST HAVE TAKEN A LOT OF COURAGE TO COME TO ME WITH THIS, ETHAN. I CAN'T PROMISE EVERYTHING'S GOING TO BE EASY, BUT WE'LL SORT THINGS OUT SOMEHOW.

IT'S NOT THAT SIMPLE, DAD. I THOUGHT I COULD CONTROL IT.

I THINK THE POLICE ARE SATISFIED JOSH WASN'T DEALING. THEY WANT HIM TO NAME HIS SUPPLIER.

▷ Josh had admitted to the police that he took drugs, but denied being the one who had given them to Tanya.

SO DID TANYA. WHAT WILL THE POLICE DO NOW?

I'VE DECIDED TO TELL THEM. FRANK DIDN'T EVEN STICK AROUND TO SEE HOW TANYA WAS.

Ethan is upset by what has happened to Tanya. It has made him aware of the risks and the dangers involved in drug-taking.

A person's decision to seek help with a drug problem may depend on different factors. Sometimes, it can take a shock to make people understand how serious the situation has become.

Ethan has now realized that he is the only person who can change his behavior. He has refused to go along with Sam. It can take a great deal of courage to stand up and face a problem, especially if you know that it will involve some pain and will not be easy. But it is never too late to decide to give up drugs. Believing in yourself is often the first step. Seeking help when you need it is a wise thing to do.

A person who is taking drugs may already be experiencing feelings of guilt or shame. Blaming someone for taking drugs will not help that person to get better, and will probably make the situation worse.

Sometimes giving support to people who are recovering from drug addiction might mean being tough on them. They may appear to be in great distress. They could even beg to be given the drug or money to buy it. Saying no to them may not be easy – at the time they may become angry or abusive. But later they will be grateful for your support.

WHAT CAN BE DONE ABOUT DRUG ABUSE?

THERE ARE MANY DIFFERENT WAYS IN WHICH PEOPLE ARE TRYING TO STOP DRUGS FROM BEING ABUSED.

It may never be possible to stop the supply of illegal drugs completely. So, as well as trying to make them less available, measures are also being taken to reduce the demand for them. Education is important in doing this. The more that people – particularly young people – know about the dangers of drugs, the less likely they might be to experiment with them. Education can also help to build self-esteem and enable you to be more assertive if you are faced with a situation in which you are being tempted to use drugs. There are many organizations which exist to help and support people with drug problems to come off the drug. Today, there is also more awareness about the need to stop some forms of drug-taking from appearing glamorous. Some pop and movie stars are involved in campaigns which help people to understand more about the dangers involved in drug-taking.

In many countries cigarette and alcohol advertising has been restricted.

Many countries have special police forces whose job it is to catch those who are trafficking in and supplying drugs. But illegal drug-taking continues to be a huge problem throughout the world.

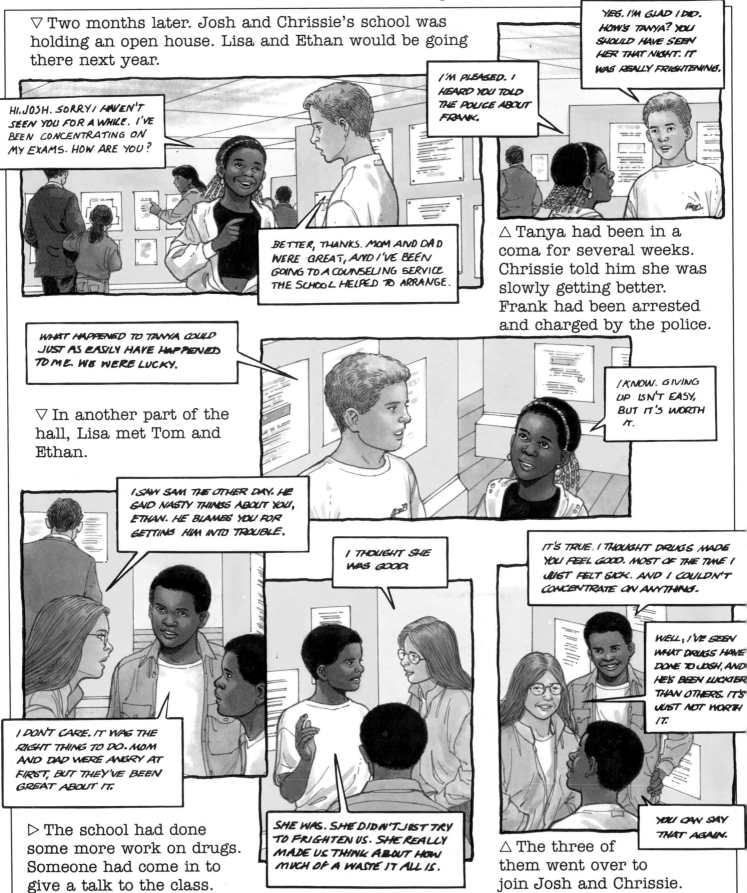

▽ Two months later. Josh and Chrissie's school was holding an open house. Lisa and Ethan would be going there next year.

HI, JOSH. SORRY I HAVEN'T SEEN YOU FOR A WHILE. I'VE BEEN CONCENTRATING ON MY EXAMS. HOW ARE YOU?

BETTER, THANKS. MOM AND DAD WERE GREAT, AND I'VE BEEN GOING TO A COUNSELING SERVICE THE SCHOOL HELPED TO ARRANGE.

I'M PLEASED. I HEARD YOU TOLD THE POLICE ABOUT FRANK.

YES. I'M GLAD I DID. HOW'S TANYA? YOU SHOULD HAVE SEEN HER THAT NIGHT. IT WAS REALLY FRIGHTENING.

△ Tanya had been in a coma for several weeks. Chrissie told him she was slowly getting better. Frank had been arrested and charged by the police.

WHAT HAPPENED TO TANYA COULD JUST AS EASILY HAVE HAPPENED TO ME. WE WERE LUCKY.

I KNOW. GIVING UP ISN'T EASY, BUT IT'S WORTH IT.

▽ In another part of the hall, Lisa met Tom and Ethan.

I SAW SAM THE OTHER DAY. HE SAID NASTY THINGS ABOUT YOU, ETHAN. HE BLAMES YOU FOR GETTING HIM INTO TROUBLE.

I DON'T CARE. IT WAS THE RIGHT THING TO DO. MOM AND DAD WERE ANGRY AT FIRST, BUT THEY'VE BEEN GREAT ABOUT IT.

I THOUGHT SHE WAS GOOD.

SHE WAS. SHE DIDN'T JUST TRY TO FRIGHTEN US. SHE REALLY MADE US THINK ABOUT HOW MUCH OF A WASTE IT ALL IS.

▷ The school had done some more work on drugs. Someone had come in to give a talk to the class.

IT'S TRUE. I THOUGHT DRUGS MADE YOU FEEL GOOD. MOST OF THE TIME I JUST FELT SICK. AND I COULDN'T CONCENTRATE ON ANYTHING.

WELL, I'VE SEEN WHAT DRUGS HAVE DONE TO JOSH, AND HE'S BEEN LUCKIER THAN OTHERS. IT'S JUST NOT WORTH IT.

YOU CAN SAY THAT AGAIN.

△ The three of them went over to join Josh and Chrissie.

Drugs can have a devastating effect on people's lives – and not just the drug taker's.
If you are tempted to take drugs when you do not need to do so for medical reasons, remember that the effect you might get from them will not last and it may not be entirely pleasant. The long-term physical and emotional effects can be extremely serious.

Whatever the problem you are faced with, it helps to talk to somebody about it.
It is important to choose somebody whom you can trust, and to whom you feel comfortable talking. If you think that somebody is dealing in drugs, or has a drug problem, it may be best to tell someone, though this might not be easy, especially if the person is a friend. Speaking out could help to save someone's life.

Learning how to stand up for your rights is a good way of protecting yourself.
Some schools have invited former drug users to talk to students about their experiences. Some schools give young people the chance to practice how they will refuse drugs, if they are ever offered them.

You always have the right to say no to drugs.

WHAT CAN WE DO?

HAVING READ THIS BOOK, YOU WILL NOW UNDERSTAND MORE ABOUT THE DIFFERENT KINDS OF DRUGS, AND THE EFFECTS THEY CAN HAVE ON PEOPLE.

All drugs can cause problems. Tobacco smoking has been linked to many major diseases, and alcohol abuse can do serious damage to people's lives.

Growing up is a time of many changes. You may be eager to try new things. People might suggest that taking drugs will make you seem more grown-up. You know that this is not the case. It is important to recognize when situations may arise in which drugs could be around. You might want to think about how you will say no if you are offered illegal drugs. If you have taken drugs already, you need to think carefully about your reasons for doing so, and what the eventual effect might be on you and those you care about. Remember that it is never too late or too early to seek help if you have a problem with drugs.

Allied Youth and Family Counseling Center
310 N. Windomere
Dallas, Texas 75208
(214) 943-1044

National Parents' Resource Institute for Drug Education (PRIDE)
10 Park Place S, Suite 540
Atlanta, GA 30303
(404) 577-4500

Reachout
14950 444th Ave. SE
North Bend, WA 98045
(206) 888-3739

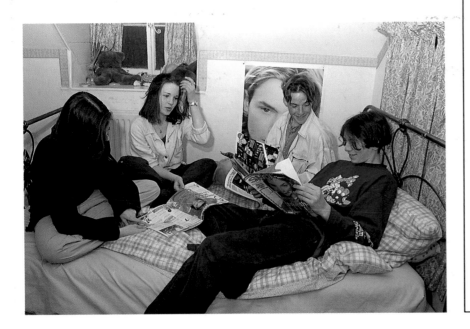

ADULTS ALSO NEED TO BE AWARE THAT CHILDREN WILL OFTEN COPY WHAT THEY ARE DOING.

If they see parents or relatives smoking or drinking, or even taking illegal drugs, they may come to think of this as acceptable behavior.
Children and adults who have read this book together may find it helpful to share their ideas and views on the issues involved. People who are experiencing problems connected with drug use might want to talk to someone who can help. The organizations listed below will be able to provide information and support, both to drug users and their families.

Pills Anonymous
P.O. Box 772
Bronx, NY 10451
718874-0700

Alateen
P.O. Box 862
Midtown Station
New York, NY 10018
(212) 302-7240
(800) 356-9996

American Council for Drug Educ. (ACDE)
136 E. 64th Street
New York, NY 10021
(800) 488-DRUG

Children of Alcoholics Foundation (COAF)
P.O. Box 4185
Grand Central Station
New York, NY 10163-4185
(212) 754-0656

Drug-Anon Focus
P.O. Box 20806
Park West Station
New York, NY 10025
(212) 484-9095

Alcoholics Anonymous World Svcs. (AA)
475 Riverside Dr.
New York, NY 10163
(212) 870-3400

"Just Say NO" International
2101 Webster St.
Suite 1300
Oakland, CA 94612
(800) 258-2766

Families Anonymous
P.O. Box 3475
Culver City, CA 90231-3475
(800) 736-9805

INDEX

Photocredits
All the pictures in this book are by Roger Vlitos except pages: 1, 3, 6 bottom, 10 bottom, 14, 15, 17 top, 17 bottom, 23 bottom, 27, 28 top: Frank Spooner; 7: Glaxo. The publishers wish to acknowledge that all of the photographs taken by Roger Vlitos in this book have been posed by models.